The Radi

Message Bottle

Writing to communicate

Tim Gray

Silver Branch Publishing

Published by Silver Branch Publishing

www.silverbranch.co.uk

ISBN 978-0-9574572-0-1

Cover art: Jaime Posadas

Design: Tim Gray

Contents

Introduction

Do you need to write in your work life? Most of us do – more than ever with the growth in online communication. Letters, emails, reports, blogs, tweets, brochures, tipsheets... There's more and more writing around us all the time – and in our personal lives too. But all this assumes that everyone can do writing well, and can just jump in and produce good work.

Writing to communicate is a skill. Maybe you've spent your life developing other skills instead – like administration or carpentry or programming or raising children. You might find all this communicating an uphill struggle. Do you wish you could do it better, with more confidence? Or maybe other people are expecting you to do it better! If so, you've come to the right place.

This book is about writing to communicate, in printed and electronic forms. Some of it may apply to spoken communication as well.

I've been doing this stuff for a long time – writing and editing newsletters, reports, websites, training packs and self-published books – and it's one of my core skills. In the last few years I've also been doing a lot of reflecting about how we communicate. My aim here is to distil that thinking into a short and, hopefully, enjoyable read that'll help you raise your game in your own communications.

We'll start with some overall principles to get you in the right mindset to craft clearer, more effective communications. As we move along we'll get more practical and look at particular areas like writing style, being persuasive and good layout. Finally we'll get tooth-gnashingly specific with a selection of common usage and grammar errors that you can quietly steer clear of in future.

(**Note:** this book is based on British English. Most of it will apply to American English as well, and to the diverse flavours of English used in other countries, but there may be some usage patterns where we part ways.)

Stars to steer by

Principles of writing to communicate

Treacherous waters

We all need to communicate – especially if we're providing services for other people. We want to get our messages out there. We don't want our audience to close the shutters before they even think about what we want to tell them. When the message gets through we don't want it to be misunderstood.

The fact is, when you send a message there's a vast array of factors that are outside your control. Here are some of the things you probably don't know or can't control about the recipients of your message:

- their attitudes and values
- the way they use language in their peer groups
- their upbringing
- their ethnic community
- their occupation
- their religious views
- their age group/generation
- what their eyesight and hearing are like
- what equipment they may be using to view or listen to your message

- their preconceptions about you, and "people like you".

They might reject your message altogether based on how they perceive it. Maybe they see signals that they shouldn't trust it, or that it's not relevant to them.

They might take it in but form an understanding that is not at all what you intended. Maybe in their circles certain words have meanings that are different from the ones you're used to.

Basically you're putting your message in a bottle, throwing it out to sea and hoping for the best.

Once you start thinking about all the things that can go wrong, it's a wonder humans ever communicate at all!

Except, of course, that there are things you *do* control. You control what you say, how you say it, and how it's presented. You can attach cunning motors to your bottle and guide it in the right direction – away from dangerous sandbanks and whirlpools and towards clear water and the next island.

Right, I think we've thrashed that metaphor within an inch of its life! To get you writing to communicate more successfully, we start by adjusting the way you think. Pass me the spanner, nurse.

Rule One

Is there one principle, above all others, that you can take on board to gain the foundation of better communication? I think there is, and this is the most boiled-down version I've come up with:

WHAT'S IN THEIR HEAD
IS NOT
WHAT'S IN YOUR HEAD

It's about realising that you have a responsibility to meet your audience at least halfway. You can't just throw some words down that you would understand yourself, presented in a way that you would find pleasant and digestible. Because they ain't you.

(You could make various parallel rule versions, like, "Their life is not your life", or even, "Their computer is not your computer". But I think the above sums it up pretty well.)

In Yorkshire, where I grew up, we sometimes said "so-and-so can't see beyond their own nose end" – meaning that all a person thought about was themselves and their own picture of the world. Someone like that can never be a great communicator. They can only appeal to people like themselves, and get frustrated when they come up against barriers.

Getting good at this requires qualities like empathy and adaptability – the ability to step outside your own worldview and habits – alongside skills in use of language and presenting information.

Of course, you can often know *something* about your audience, especially if you're targeting a particular sort of person. That lets you get at least partly into their mindset and adjust accordingly. But making your work accessible to a general audience as well is usually a good thing.

Two powerful questions

When planning a piece of communication, ask these questions.

- Who is it aimed at?
- What do you want to happen as a result?

That will tell you all sorts of things about the language to use and the key points to make.

Who is it aimed at?

If you have a specific audience group, think about what their key concerns are, and how they talk about them. What terms can you use to frame your points; what buzzwords can you hit? If it's a group you don't have a feel for, hit some websites and see if you can find a common tone.

For example, an organisation for small businesses operating in a locality will probably be a bit conservative and focus on practical stuff with money talk in the foreground. A national alliance of solo entrepreneurs working in life coaching and therapies may use more touchy-feely language with an emphasis on clients and wellbeing, with money talk in the background.

There's a trend for people to say all communications must be targeted. I think "targeted at everyone" is a very valid answer. It's just that when the audience is wide, the demand for clarity is greater and you have to pull back to simple, clear language.

Actually I would argue that, regardless of your audience right now, you should try to find a platform of simple, clear language that also conveys your distinctive voice, and make that your communication core.

If you get that right, most people will respond well and you'll have a lot of flexibility to do different things. It may involve getting rid of some bad habits!

What do you want to happen?

You might want your audience to:

- learn new stuff for the sake of interest (perhaps for a hobby)
- gain information that will help them to cope with a type of situation if/when it happens
- improve their skills
- change their behaviour or thinking habits
- campaign for change

- join something
- buy a product or service.

Whatever it is will affect the language and presentation to use. Informing is different from persuading. A group that's already bought in is very different from one that's resistant.

A group of railway enthusiasts will be happy to listen to train stories. People on a first aid course could range from interested in gaining skills to resenting being forced to go. People looking for life-changing coaching are raring to go, if they can find the right person (at a price they can afford).

So you need to plan your communication to sell the benefits up front and close the deal at the end. Going back to Rule One, you can't assume that the people you're addressing are as interested in your thing as you are. Hook their attention and lead them toward your outcome.

Do you throw a newsletter full of info at people if the outcome you want is for them to lobby the government? Probably not, though it might be useful as support for the campaign. Give them just enough info to trigger their interest, ask them to take the action (making it as easy as possible), tell them how to get more info if they want it, and don't take up any more of their time. That's working very well for online campaigning communities like Avaaz and 38 Degrees – taking tiny nibbles of individuals' attention and aggregating them into powerful levers for shared values.

Total communication

Let's try a quick exercise with an experience you can probably relate to. Imagine this.

You receive a letter from a bank, utility company or local council. It mistypes your name and gets your title wrong (like Mr instead of Ms or vice versa). It's badly laid out, and you spot several misspellings. The writer says things like, "Notwithstanding the aforementioned communications from yourself, at this moment in time..." The letter doesn't answer the question(s) you actually asked when you wrote to the organisation. You're not entirely sure what it *is* saying.

How does this make you feel?

Consciously or unconsciously, do you pick up any of these?

- This person/organisation doesn't care about me.
- This person/organisation doesn't care about doing a good job.
- This person/organisation is incompetent.
- This person/organisation is out to screw me over.

Does that letter make you feel good about your relationship with the organisation? Of course not. You'll probably spread the story of how rubbish it is. You may even decide to take your business elsewhere. And the story that spreads is "Blobington Assistance Services did this to me", not "Bob the bored junior clerical officer wrote a dodgy letter".

Think total

Everything you put out to an audience sends messages about you or your organisation. Reports, blog posts, emails, tweets, letterheads, business cards...

In our brains, a small department is processing what you are saying. At the same time the larger network of the Social Intelligence Service swings into action, combing every tiny cue for information about who you are and what you intend. Warm colours or cool colours? Cramped archaic-looking type, or overblown flourishes trying to claim all the space on the page? Informative or cryptic? Trying to score points by suggesting we are inferior? Bored jobsworth who can't be bothered to write something decent... or maybe just a bit stupid? Or is it pleasant, helpful, attractively presented and generally giving the impression that we the readers are important to the author?

EVERYTHING YOU PUT OUT IS
AN AMBASSADOR FOR YOU

So give it some nice choccies to hand out!

I've found that some people simply don't have it on their radar that *presentation matters*. They stream a dense assemblage of words into a word processor document, and out it goes to the recipient. That can be a particular issue in large, bureaucratic organisations where there are loads of documents flying around. When people have no choice but to read your stuff, maybe it's easier to justify to yourself not taking any trouble over it.

But it's all building up an impression somewhere in the minds of colleagues, clients and partner organisations. You might as well take a portion of your marketing budget and set fire to it.

Personal branding

This is a new label for these issues, gaining profile rapidly in an age when so many of us are visible to the world on the internet. The commercial/marketing association of "branding" can put some people off, but it does refer to something important.

An often-used quote from Jeff Bezos, founder of Amazon, puts it well: "Your brand is what people say about you when you are not in the room." When people think of you, what qualities and associations go along with that in their minds? Obviously we want them to be positive ones! It's a bit similar to ideas like "reputation" and "character".

People will always associate *something* with you, so you do have a personal brand whether you pay any attention to managing it or not. It's especially important for small businesses in the online age, because with so many products and services spread out before them, people choose to trade with those that embody qualities they value and identify with.

Your communications form an important part of this. When you're not there in person they are your representatives. When you *are* there in person, they've set the other party's expectations.

So the total communication approach involves planning your brand, and thinking about what your message bottles say about you. Even if you don't have a detailed picture of a distinctive brand, you want to hit buttons like smart, professional, thorough and friendly. You don't want to get labelled as sloppy, uneducated, or not really interested in your readers or your work.

Make your stuff simple but good, and be aware enough to spot unintended impressions and iron them out. I've seen a website *about* personal branding that instantly got labelled in my head as "cluttered and confusing". Do you think that raised or lowered my trust in those guys' expertise?

Honouring the work

It's vital that you value what you're writing.

That could be because you have an emotional investment in it. Perhaps it's something you've been working on for a long time, or something you really want to share with the world.

Otherwise, you need to apply your professionalism: the word warrior's way. You're going to take pride in doing the work to the best of your ability, and then move on to the next thing.

Because if you don't care about producing good work, you're likely to produce bad work. It requires attention to detail. Some people naturally have more of that than others. (I have lots myself, but am weaker in other areas like tying my shoelaces.) If writing is a skill you have to work at, it's doubly important that you honour the work because you're more likely to slip. But even if it's one of your core skills, going on autopilot can lead to silly mistonks.

Know your skills

Who are the worst writers? The people who can't do it but think they can and won't be told otherwise. Someone who knows their skills aren't great can improve, or get help from other people. Someone who insists they're great does neither, and keeps sending out stuff that makes their organisation look bad.

Because most of us (in the developed countries at least) learn to write at school, it's easy to assume that everybody can do it. But writing basically, then properly, then well – these are levels of skill, the same as any other activity.

Different people have different skills. That's just a fact. If someone's not a great writer, perhaps they're a brilliant speaker, or a super-competent administrator, or a wonderful parent. There's no value judgment involved. There's just a very practical question: when you need to write communications material, what level are your skills at and how can you apply that?

I suggest that as a message-bottle-sender, you're responsible for taking a clear, honest look at your own skills and working out how to produce good communication *starting from where you are.*

Good doesn't mean fancy. Let's get this out of the way: big clever words are not big and they're not clever! You may have seen stuff by academics and officials that shows off knowing lots of words and being able to construct long, complicated sentences. But could you understand it? I say that producing simple, clear, effective communications is a greater skill. Plus, the more fancy words and punctuation someone uses, the more likely it is that they'll come unstuck by using them incorrectly.

Checking. Any substantial and important piece of writing needs to be checked before it goes on its way. That requires the skills to know what needs fixing, and enough mental distance from the work to be able to spot errors when you read it. If you have a good level of skill in this area you can check your own work after an hour or two, or after leaving it overnight. Most people need to get someone else to look at it. This is where you need to be honest with yourself. If you think you can proofread your own work and you really can't, the finished product won't be the best it can be.

Know when to bring in help. Be the manager of your work. If you know there are areas where your skills aren't great, bring someone with those skills on to your team. That could be a friend or someone you hire, as long as they're good, objective, and pleasant to work with. Even better, if they explain the reasons behind the changes they suggest you can build up your own skills in the process.

Writing the message

Style and process

Style

The words you choose and the way you put sentences and paragraphs together combine to make an overall shape, and that shape is the voice your readers perceive for you. As we've seen, the way you write can make a big difference to how easy it is to get your message across, and readers will also be extracting clues to decide whether to like and trust you.

So, what sort of writing style do you want to have? Here are some common baseline styles to think about.

Academic style

When you're working in academic circles (or perhaps specialist teams in other settings), one of the key payoffs of your writing can be to show people how clever you are. It's a natural social status thing, but it can lead to some peculiar writing. There's a perceived reward for using big words, complicated sentences and jargon. Now jargon can be a very useful thing, for speeding up communication between people in a particular field. But you need to be able to adapt to a different style of writing when communicating to a more general audience.

Bureaucratic style

This includes a lot of unnecessarily long words, convoluted language and clichéd phrases.

"At the end of the day, the company will deliver a world-class service to yourself."

or

"We will help you."

This style is common among people working in business and the public sector. I think that's because they've seen it in communications they've had from organisations, so they think it's the right way to do things. But really, it just looks like struggling to control cumbersome language that they're not comfortable with.

I say it's more respectful to customers and colleagues to take the time to communicate clearly and concisely. Then they can absorb your message quickly and move on to their next thing.

Poetic style

This uses lots of highly descriptive language, with plenty of metaphor and other stuff thrown in. Doing it well is a brilliant skill for poetry and some kinds of fiction: it's great at evoking emotions and pulling sensory impressions from the reader's memory. It's not great, though, for communication that's trying to get points across effectively and efficiently.

Journalistic style

This is a better model for most communication. I don't mean making everything a headline.

> "Nottingham customer in tax refund shocker!"
> "Life coach helped me focus, says mum of 3!"

I mean the way the writing is clear and concise because space is precious. The story is competing with others in the publication, and the reader has to be able to skim it and zoom in where they're interested, so journalists have to trim the fat. They're also good at putting the key points first: editors tend to "cut from the bottom", so the material expanding on aspects of the story has to be expendable.

You might want to try rewriting a piece (your own or grabbed from elsewhere) in this trimmed-down style.

Your style

Alongside writing *well*, and to suit your audience, you have to write as *you*. We want to hear what you have to say, in your voice. Do you have one? Do you know what its qualities are?

If you haven't done much writing it may take time to evolve, and pass through phases of mimicking other writers. If you've written for a while, your style has probably developed unconsciously. It should flow naturally; but it may be worth doing a bit of conscious fine-tuning. What does your audience say about it? Do you have any habits that are off-putting or jarring? Are you holding back from expressing yourself fully?

When people tell you they like the way you write, you've got something! And when they do, they'll want to read more. A great writing voice is a treasured experience.

Pause for power

Have you ever seen a piece of writing that goes on and on without a break or even any punctuation and you get tired reading it and lose your place in the sentence and then it goes on to talk about something else like using colons and semi-colons or the price of fish and you're just about ready to give up?

That's obviously not a good way to write! Particularly so when you're writing to communicate. You're trying to get ideas and skills from the page into your reader's head. So ideally you want each sentence to be about one idea. Then pause so they can take a second to digest it. Then move on to the next link in your chain. That also helps to navigate the text if they come back after a break, or if they backtrack to remind themselves of a previous point.

You can apply the same principle to paragraph breaks. That makes an even clearer step from one set of ideas to the next.

Have you ever watched people speaking in public and compared their techniques? Imagine someone who rabbits on in a continuous stream, keeping their eyes on their notes. Now imagine someone who delivers their points at a measured speed, with frequent pauses, looking up to make eye contact with the audience. The second one might not get through as much content in the time, but it's way more likely to have an impact on the audience and stick in their minds. You can apply this to your writing too – and you don't have to stand in front of an audience!

However, be aware that using a lot of short sentences turns into a particular kind of style. That second paragraph above is heading in this direction. It's a bit machine-gun-like, sort of barky and in-your-face. It's particularly useful when you want to bring the reader up short and confront them with something, but if overused it can get a bit tiring and annoying.

In general, aim for natural-sounding sentences so stuff about length and structure fades into the background and the reader just feels that you're easy to follow.

Writing for the web

Publishing channels like websites and blogs make it easy to throw information on to the screen and shovel it out to readers. So people do; and there are a lot of bad web pages out there. Like anything else, it needs a touch of skill and consideration.

Making your points through short, snappy paragraphs is good for informative writing in print, but on the web it's *essential*. When reading on screen, there's less text to view at once, reading it is harder work, and we're accustomed to being fed short bursts of info.

So if you think it might be good to break a paragraph, it probably is. And you need to develop good technical skills so you can write accurately in a journalistic style while presenting a distinctive voice.

You also need to think about making it *connected* – with links for following up important terms or sources, or funky added value. Using "click here" is very outdated. It's much better to make actual descriptive terms clickable – like "Jane Jones has written a useful piece about <u>the role of ducks in cities</u>." That also helps visually-impaired people who are using software to read the page aloud, as it makes it clear what the link's about, whereas a list of "click here" links is unhelpful.

On humour

A touch of humour can really liven up a text. It helps to convey the impression of a real human being behind the words, with experience of the absurdity we call life, and the wit and wisdom to reflect on it.

But this is a hard thing to get right – as the actress said to the bishop. If it's not a natural thing for you to do and you try to force it, it'll fall flat. You can work it in a bit more stealthily by using absurd analogies and including anecdotes that pull in other people's humour.

If humour really isn't you at all, don't feel compelled to use it. There are other ways to show personality in your writing – like integrity that shines through, or having passed through the fire and brought back quiet wisdom.

Even if you can do it well, humour is an extremely subjective thing. It varies between individuals, groups and even nationalities. I've had the experience of releasing a "humorous" book and having it fall flat with many Americans because it was too British – which I think meant that it used puns and allusion and sarcasm rather than being obvious and in-your-face. So you have to be prepared for a certain quota of those tumbleweed moments. It helps if the work is aimed at a particular audience whose tastes you can predict – or if you already have a following that buys into your personal style.

Make sure you're actually being funny, and in a way the audience will like. I don't meant smart-alec remarks or putting everything down with "witty" sarcasm. Maybe some comedians with an established style and following can sell that, but in general it's likely to leave the reader annoyed or depressed. I once bought a TV listings magazine, where it turned out every programme entry was a "clever" sarcastic sideswipe. Never bought that again.

Watch your offensiveness factor. Personally I don't like swearing and innuendo (though you may have noticed me indulging myself earlier) – but a bit of it can work for specific audiences. If you buy a collection of opinion pieces by a modern comedian, you pretty much expect a level of sweariness. If you buy a self-help book about calming your life down, you don't. When in doubt, leave it out.

Inclusive language

By this I mean word choice and usage with a greater awareness of the power of words to be hurtful or unfair to groups of people, and to reinforce negative attitudes towards them. The aim is to replace these with patterns that treat them respectfully and considerately.

Some people may have a reflex to think, "Huh, political correctness, nonsense." Perhaps especially if they consume certain kinds of media. If so, please reread the previous paragraph. If you really think those are bad things, you are not someone I'm writing for. I hope, rather, that you'll be willing to give it some thought without the baggage it's acquired.

This is something that's only really developed in the last few decades, as we've become more aware of the need to treat all people equally, and disenfranchised groups have been reclaiming their power. It's a fast-moving field, and that's created a lot of conflict: people's language patterns have been laid down over many years, and asking them to change instantly can provoke a defensive response. There have also been well-documented attempts to apply principles without proper understanding and forethought, producing some silly results and damaging public perception of the process.

I hope you will feel the goals are worth a bit of reflection and research to refine your own writing. You don't have to change your entire voice and vocabulary overnight: in any case the field is in its adolescence and the specifics will keep changing for a while yet. The main thing is to be open to having your views changed. You may get picked up on words that you've been using for years with no bad intent. It's understandable to go on the defensive – especially if the person is passionate about their cause – but it's much better if everyone involved can stay calm and share understanding of what's behind it.

I can't go into great detail here, but let's look at some examples. One key principle is to emphasise that people with problems are still people, with their own dignity. So "disabled people" is being replaced by "people with disabilities" – or even "people with physical impairments", which makes no judgement on whether these cause them trouble in interacting with the world. "Older people" is preferred to "the elderly". The old term "spastic", which became rather an emotionally-charged label, has been replaced by "person with cerebral palsy". "Cerebral palsy sufferer" isn't good because it judges their relationship with their illness and makes them sound like a victim.

If you're writing within or for the voluntary sector, you'll face a particular expectation of making your language inclusive according to current thinking. People you're working with should be able to help if necessary.

His and hers

This is probably the most common example of inclusive language. In the past, if you were referring to a person whose sex was unknown – perhaps as a generic example – you would write them as male.

- The reader is free to make use of this example as he sees fit.

Today we know that this is discrimination against women and we need a fairer way. Unfortunately English doesn't contain a pronoun to refer to a single person generically. So writers have tied themselves in knots trying to find a compromise. Perhaps the most common version is this:

- The reader is free to make use of this example as he or she sees fit.

That's technically fine, but it makes sentences a bit cumbersome. If a piece of writing makes lots of generic references, it can get very clunky indeed. You also get the "I hope it is helpful to him or her". Occasionally you'll see "he/she" or even "s/he", which is pitchforks and torches time. I've also seen books where the general pronoun alternates between sections: “he” in chapter 1, “she” in chapter 2, and so on. Other writers have shared them between roles: the generic player or guest is “he” and the generic referee or host is “she”.

All of these are ignoring the fact that there is a standard way of doing it and, although it’s not perfect, it’s better than those as long as it’s applied intelligently. You use “they”.

- The reader is free to make use of this example as they see fit.

Now of course “they” is the plural pronoun, drafted in. Some people get hung up on that – especially because you need to make surrounding words agree with the plural even though you’re using it for a singular. Above, I used “see” rather than “sees”. That’s pretty innocuous, but sometimes it can get a little ugly. If that happens, change the sentence to keep it generic and get the meaning across more smoothly. With our example that’s trivial:

- Readers are free to make use of this example as they see fit.

Here’s an example of a trickier one.

- The reader should try this out themselves/themself.

"Themselves" is a very heavily plural word, so it doesn't work, and "themself" isn't a word at all. A bit of lateral thinking is required!

- You should try this out yourself.
- The reader should try this out personally.

The editing process

Once you've got your draft text, it needs some level of editing before it is unleashed on the world. The publishing industry uses a range of terms for specific roles within a very robust editing process, like "proofreading" and "copy editing". Broadly:

- proofreading is spotting typing errors, grammar mistakes, and stuff like that
- editing is getting more involved with the writer, suggesting ways to move things around to change the structure, querying the way things are worded, etc.

You can probably lump it all together unless you're dealing with professionals in the field. If it's your own document and you're checking it yourself (or having it checked), it's the process of refining the draft so it's the best it can be. The larger and more important the work, the more important checking becomes. This is part of the craft of writing. If you submit an article to a magazine, for instance, the editor wants to see that you know your stuff and won't require loads of patching-up from their team.

Many people find that getting their thoughts down is a very different thinking mode from pruning and polishing. You may find it best to divide your time into one or the other: separate your capturing ideas head from your editing head, so you can get fully into the rhythm of each.

For editing you have to be tough and ruthless. Kind of like a pirate with a sniper rifle… But it makes the difference between writing that could have been great and writing that actually *is*.

Perspective

The most important thing with editing is *distance*. You have to be able to look at the text from an objective perspective. If you've just finished working on it, you don't have that, especially if you've reworked it a lot. Mistakes can stare you in the face and you won't see them. Your mind is full of the shining ideal as-it-should-be version, and will paper over any discrepancies.

You need to take a break and *let your mind settle*. Go and do normal things for a while! How long? That's hugely variable, depending on the length of the work, how focused you've been, and what your editing skills are like. If you're good at it, you could come back to a short article within an hour. In many cases overnight is good: sleep refreshes the perspective.

Reading the text aloud to yourself can be very helpful in spotting mistakes, especially clumsy phrasing. I think it puts your brain in a slightly different mode from scanning the page visually.

Software tools can be helpful and frustrating at the same time. Spellcheckers highlight any word they don't know. It's worth paying attention in case you've mistyped something. Grammar checkers are trying to do something extremely complicated which is better handled by a human brain, and highlight a lot of sentences that are perfectly fine. Develop your own skills and you can ignore them.

An important mindset skill is the willingness to "*kill your darlings*". Maybe a section of text was part of a beautiful, elegant theoretical framework. Maybe you worked long and hard on it. But as the work as a whole takes shape, that section ends up not fitting in, or not doing a useful job, or distracting the reader from the main point. You have to be objective and adaptable enough to say "oh well" and cut it out. Of course, there's no reason you can't copy it into a file somewhere in case it's useful for something you do in the future.

Working with an editor

If you think you'll *never* be able to look at the work objectively, *get someone else* on board to help. It's probably a good idea to get someone else's input anyway, especially for something long and important, because *editing your own work is hard*. It's often said that many well-known writers owe their reputation to good editors!

For most people, a good process is to do an editing pass yourself to catch whatever you can spot, and then pass it to someone with a fresher eye.

This person shouldn't just be one of your mates who'll agree to do it! I've seen supposedly proofread work that's full of errors. That's just making the process longer for no gain.

It needs to be someone who *actually has the skills*. If you want professional results, you may need to pay someone. It's not cheap, but it's an investment in your work.

They have to be able to work with a high degree of accuracy, to your timescale. Ideally they'll be able to suggest good wording where yours is a bit uncertain. You need to be able to work together constructively, but it's also handy if their viewpoint is different from yours so they can challenge you a bit, like helping you think about different audience groups or pushing you to sort out woolly parts of the text.

Calling for help

Writing persuasively

Write, camera, action!

As well as writing to inform, you can write to get people to do something: adopt a view, change behaviour, write to their MP, sign up to a mailing list, buy a product or service. Here are some thoughts that will help.

Remember the Two Powerful Questions from earlier?

- Who is it aimed at?
- What do you want to happen as a result?

Those are particularly important here. Any clues you can gather will help you fine-tune your message.

Rule 1a

THEY DON'T CARE ABOUT YOUR STUFF
LIKE YOU CARE ABOUT YOUR STUFF

This kind of falls out of Rule One, but it's worth hammering it home. I bet that, like me, you've had the experience of somebody talking to you about something they're enthusiastic, even passionate, about – but failing to make the bridge to why you should be interested in it too.

To them, they've internalised the greatness of the thing so that *obviously* everyone else will see it too, and your lack of engagement frustrates them. To you, this person has just parachuted into your life and is expecting you to jump straight in to something you've never even thought about before, and you want to defend your space.

What's the lesson for your writing? You can't assume the reader's interest. You have to earn it. Sell the benefits; draw out the points; bring them along with you. Respect filtering. Make your key points briefly and let them ask for more if they want to. Write your stuff well enough that you end up with the readers who actually want what you have to say.

Don't lecture

If you just tell people to change behaviour or take an action or take on board the facts you present, the take-up will be very small. Humans have the capacity for rational, reflective thought – but most of us, most of the time, don't operate in that mode. We run on habits, and an entrenched picture of the world. That's been kind of handy for getting us past the "hungry tiger, run away" stage! But it doesn't serve us so well in today's complex world when we really ought to have a proper think about a bunch of important issues rather than a set of kneejerk reactions.

The fact is that if you start telling people the way they do things is wrong, the worldview in their head will outright reject the input or they'll interpret it as criticism, a form of attack. They get defensive, the shutters come down and you've lost. You need to give yourself the best chance of getting through this minefield. That means starting from where they are, giving them a message they can relate to and drawing them with you.

As an example: the early environmental movement produced lots of *informative* material about the issues and expected that to lead to behaviour change and campaign action. For people with certain kinds of thinking styles, it did, because they went very logically from a description of a problem to a need to solve it. The majority of the population went unswayed. Twenty-odd years on, the movement has more marketing savvy and continues to improve its understanding of behaviour and attitudes.

Two big levers

The book *Influencer* by a group of behaviour change researchers (see end notes) looks at strategies that have been successful around the world in changing people's behaviour. It's mostly about working directly with groups, but we can certainly learn a thing or two. The authors suggest focusing down to just a few "vital behaviours" to change. Then when you're presenting a different way to do things, there are just two key questions for which you need to provide answers: "Can I do it?" (ability) and "Will it be worth it?" (motivation).

For the first, show how achievable it is and put the first step right in front of them – click here for an ebook or tipsheet, write to your MP at this address, etc. "Hundreds of people like you have quit smoking with the help of our support programme."

For the second, "sell the sizzle" – paint a picture of the better world that waits on the other side of this change. "I quit smoking five years ago. I feel better than I have in years, and I can do things with my young grandchildren."

Tell stories

Human beings are wired for stories. We always look for patterns in things, and isolated facts don't fit that as well as a memorable narrative. We're social creatures too, so hearing about things happening to people engages us. There can be less savoury things at play as well, of course, like wanting to feel better about ourselves compared to that stupid/obnoxious/unfortunate person. And of course we tend to be self-centred, which means bits of our brain are busy trying to make links between the story and our own life – which helps to make the message effective.

The authors of *Influencer* talk about how unhelpful verbal persuasion – telling people to do things – can be. It's much more powerful if we *experience* the alternate way of doing things. They give the example of a group of American workers trying the corresponding job in a Japanese factory that's much more productive than theirs, and finding they can do it.

Often it's not possible to provide the direct experience. Then, say the authors, provide a *vicarious experience*: watching someone else having the experience, or getting drawn into a story about someone having it, activates stuff in our brains in a similar way to having the experience ourselves. Only a few workers from the

American factory could go to Japan. They had to find a story of their experience that their colleagues could trust in order to spread the idea of improving work practices. So a good story really helps the reader to see that the change is possible and worthwhile things come from making the effort.

Stories tend to be more powerful when they're about individuals rather than groups. We relate to individuals: and it's easier to build up a personal picture that can hook us. That's why organisations like to use case studies of individuals who have had problems or experienced a benefit.

A strong start

Want an opener that draws people in and makes them keep reading? Here are a few tactics. Some of them overlap. You could use more than one, but don't overload the reader. Pick a direction that's right for the work and authentic for you.

The demonstration of empathy. You say something that really makes them feel you understand the need or gap or curiosity that brought them to your work. "Wouldn't you like to be free of this debilitating and embarrassing problem once and for all?"

The brilliant utterance. If you can put something so well that it sticks in the reader's mind, and perhaps sums things up in a way they hadn't quite thought of before, they'll carry on to see what more you've got. You may even be able to do this with a quote from someone else that's really appropriate to your theme.

The engaging style. If you're a good writer with a distinctive style/voice (one that people like, not an over-smart or annoying one), that may be a pleasant enough experience to carry the reader along.

The true confession. You open up details of your own life, and how your experience relates to your theme. The point is to make it a story, so that the reader wants to follow through to the end. It's good for creating an emotional connection, though be careful about how much personal detail you share with people you've never met.

The intriguing question. You ask a question, or give an anecdote that raises one ("what could possibly be happening?") – something that gets the reader's curiosity twitching so that they have to read on for the answer. This is easier if you can define your audience and hit their interest buttons.

The perspective shift. Within a few words, you make the reader look at the topic from a different angle – or even upside down. This cracks open their understanding, perhaps making familiar territory new again, and they'll be keen for you to lead them through it. (It has to be a perspective that actually makes sense and leads to useful insight, not just a crazy theory with no foundation.)

All of the above are just openers. If they go on too long, the reader might conclude that you don't have anything useful to tell them after all. Follow up quickly with nice digestible content that shows you really are going to help them with their stuff. The opener can turn into a repeated theme throughout the piece, though, re-emphasising your insight, sympathy or whatever.

Language and rapport

Can you identify topics, words, sentence patterns and styles that your target audience would use? Mirror some of that back to them to foster a sense of similarity and "people-like-me". It makes a big difference to whether they trust what you have to say.

Have you ever been at a gathering where you're talking to different people and learning a bit about their work, hobbies and home life? I've found that if I can show I know just a little bit about an area that's important to them, that instantly strengthens rapport. For instance, if someone turns out to be a printer I can draw on limited experience of small print jobs to speak just a bit in their own language. I'm not misrepresenting myself as being a specialist like them – I'd soon be found out anyway! – but I've acquired some "people-like-me" points.

This is harder in writing because the conversation is one-way with no feedback. But you can drop little subtle hooks that you think might get a bite – especially if you have a clear audience group. "A few years ago when I worked in the office of a national charity, I spotted a common thread in the way different teams organised their work." I just pinged people who've worked in an office, who've worked in teams, and who are interested in charities and the voluntary sector. Now they're primed for me to say something insightful that they can relate to their lives.

You can maintain this impression of connection by throwing in occasional hooks that relate to the way your audience speaks and writes internally – like "line manager" or "relationship marketing" or "carbon footprint".

However, I wouldn't get drawn too far away from the simple, clear style you have (I hope!) been working to develop. The world has many management-speak wafflers, and too few clear communicators. Make occasional excursions into the foothills of jargon; just enough to remind the reader that you understand them, but not enough to confuse other readers who don't know their world.

That's the downside of using language hooks for particular audiences, of course – other readers are liable to get turned off. Juggle your rapport carefully.

Build agreement

If you get the reader in the habit of agreeing with you on easy things, they'll be more likely to go along with you on harder sells. You get a foot in their worldview as "people-I-agree-with". So it can be handy to spot potential sticky points for your audience and lead up to them with this in mind.

In a condensed piece of communication like a web page introducing your business, you can include a list of "yes statements" that any reader is likely to answer with a mental nod.

- "Would you like to double your income in three months?" That's pretty hard for anyone to say no to!
- "Do you want to discover the secrets that have already made hundreds of people richer?" Hell yes, why should those guys get all the good stuff?
- "Do you want your website to be attractive, easy to use and effective in communicating your messages and brand?" It'd be an odd site if you didn't.

After a few of these, your pitch for a £1500 weekend seminar might just get a foot in the door because it's harder to shift to saying no. Asking straight out for a valuable weekend and a lot of money definitely wouldn't get very far! (It's more realistic to continue the yes chain with a low-cost product or service and build up gradually.)

Establishing yourself as "people-like-me" is very similar to this. Having established yourself as someone the reader relates to, and someone who has helped them, they're less likely to reject what you say.

A word of warning. Lots of people are aware of this technique, so it's very widespread. And some people go on and on – like those great long landing pages on the web where they take 27 screenfuls to sell you their event. So your readers may already be overexposed, and tire of it easily. Keep it concise and not too in-your-face.

Form the right expectation up front

Most people find it difficult to deal with thwarted expectations. They'll take in information and incorporate it into their worldview, their internal picture of how things are. Worldviews are highly unreasonable and defensive beasts, and can exert a powerful influence over our behaviour. If presented with data that conflicts with their worldview, a person will at least become uncomfortable. Some people can adapt quite easily. Others might refuse to accept the conflicting data, or argue about it, or even become aggressive, depending on what's at stake.

So it's a good idea to avoid that unpleasantness by being as clear as possible up front.

Here's an example. I just got a flyer through the door about a local exercise class. The flyer hasn't been professionally designed, and there are several things that could be improved. One thing I notice is that the people on the photos are all women. It doesn't say in the text that it's women only. Let's imagine a possible situation. You're a man who's drawn in by the keywords. You're pleased that it's close to where you live, and go along to give it a try. At the door you're told that it's for women only and you can't come in.

Speedbump! How do you feel about that? Can you adapt, or do you react against it somehow? It's also possible that the women there don't deal with it very well, because in their heads *of course* it's for women only, and what's this bloke up to? All of which could be avoided by a few words on the flyer.

It's easier to set people on the right course at the start than to change their momentum later. Rule One again! How might someone who isn't you perceive your message?

Ask for what you want

Don't forget to spell out very clearly the thing that you want people to do! It's easy to assume that readers can tell what you're getting at from your text. But remember Rule One! People will find all sorts of creative interpretations if there's any room to do so. (Surveys and feedback forms are the worst things I've seen for this. You get some amazing interpretations of your instructions.)

Try leaving your text for a while, then come back and see if you still think it's clear.

In most cases you should have a paragraph that stands on its own and says, "Do this, and here's the step you need to take to do it." You could have two or three paragraphs at different points in the text, saying it in different ways. I wouldn't keep banging on about it though, as it starts to look like a hard sell and that puts people off. Lead them to an appropriate point and then deliver the punchline.

Labelling the bottle

Layout and design

Styles and structure

Styles (as a technical term, distinct from your writing style) are a really useful feature you'll find in most software used for preparing documents. The program may even give you templates with styles already set up.

A style is a set of formatting instructions attached to a label like "Heading 1". You can stick that label on a block of text, and all that formatting will be applied to it: font, size, colour, spacing, and so on. This is the best way to lay out a document, because:

- it makes formatting consistent throughout the document – all Heading 1 text is the same
- if you want to make changes ("Heading 1 should be a bit bigger") you can tweak the settings for a style and they'll be applied to every piece of text with that label on it.

By **structure** I mean the way the text is broken up into paragraphs, different heading levels, and so on. It organises the text and breaks it up, making it easier to follow. It's best to have a nice simple structure, then it'll be easy for you and the readers to keep track of where you are.

Here's an example that works for structure and layout in most documents, though you'll always have to tweak settings a bit. (It refers to "points" as a unit of text size, but you can just read those bits as "enough of a size difference to be visually distinct".)

- Body text (often styled as "Normal") – a well-made typeface that's clear to read and a decent size. You can use bold and italic within it for emphasis. I tend to use bold as mini-headings for paragraphs, or to introduce new terms, and italics for stressing words. Underline may be best avoided as it can be confused with web links.
- Heading 3 – for sub-sections, breaking up sections – 2 points bigger than the body text – can be the body typeface in bold, or a different heading typeface that contrasts with the body text – something attractive with decent emphasis.
- Heading 2 – for sections, where you talk about a given subject – 4 points bigger than the body text, in the heading typeface.
- Heading 1 – for main sections or parts of the work – like Heading 2 but 6-8 points bigger than the body text.
- Main title – a possible extra for the whole document – like Heading 1 but bigger.

- Bullet – body text plus indents and spacing set to look good with your layout scheme.

Do use **paragraph breaks** to make a clear separation between one idea and the next. When you edit, watch out for places where you change tack mid-paragraph, and ask yourself whether to put a break in. Do use headings to separate major themes in the same way.

Pick the font for the job

Each font has its own strong points, and its own character on the page. That will colour the perception of your document. For ebooks that are read on e-reader devices you may not have any control over this, but for other documents the font is a vital part of the design.

The language is a bit confusing here. Technically a **typeface** is a family like "Arial", whose members like "Arial Regular" and "Arial Bold" are **fonts**. (The terms come from back when letters were on separate metal pieces, put together to make a page for print.) I'm just going to use "font", as that's what your computer will be calling them.

Most people have loads on their computer already, installed along with various bits of software. You can also buy more at sites like *fonts.com* and *myfonts.com*. Another good resource is *identifont.com*, which helps you find fonts by their properties, or fonts that are similar to one whose name you know.

Sometimes the distinction between fonts is very subtle, and if you compare a word or two you won't see it. I occasionally set up a document to help me, by copying and pasting multiple versions of a paragraph, then formatting each in a different font and printing the page out to see which of the possibles is best for a project. Comparing blocks of text helps you see tall or squat, heavy or light, modern or classic.

Don't use too many fonts, or excessively fancy fonts. Elegant simplicity is best, with one for body text, one for headings, and maybe another for occasional emphasis like boxed text.

The body font should be very readable – not a wacky decorative one! – and well-constructed so it displays well at different sizes and in bold and italic.

Not everyone agrees, and it's not a universal rule, but for a print document you probably want a **serif** font – one with the little cross-strokes at the ends of letters – as those are easier for the eye in large doses. For contrast, it's common to use a **sans serif** font (no cross-strokes) for headings. For web pages, viewed on a screen with much lower resolution than print, the simplicity of sans serif type often works better.

Don't overuse common fonts. In the PC world, Times New Roman and Arial are the old stagers. They're very well-made fonts, but because readers have seen them so much they have the connotation of being old-fashioned and boring. (I mean for print or PDF work: Arial is still a good choice for websites.) Picking a slightly different serif or sans serif font will liven up your work.

Font licensing

If you're going to buy a font from one of the sales sites, watch out for the licensing terms that come with the purchase. These will probably be viewable from a very small and subtle link shortly before you check out. They may be written in a way that's unjustifiably hard to understand. Different font creation companies ("foundries") give you different rights to use their work. They may expect you to pay extra for some things, like using the font in the layout of a product that's going to be sold commercially.

I bring this up because it happened to me recently. I'd got attached to a font that was a brilliant fit for a project, then realised I couldn't use it commercially. I enquired, and when eventually the sales site understood what I was asking it offered a licence for *ten times* the original cost, a few hundred dollars – a killer for a small project. The foundry's agents had a rather better deal, roughly the same amount as the original, repeatable for each product using the font. In the end I found another font not quite as good with a reasonable one-off do-what-you-want fee.

You may say, "Why not just use it? How would they ever know?" Well, apart from being dishonest it builds a risk into the project. I'd rather get the design right up front than be forced to change it somewhere down the line, along with other possible unpleasantness.

Fonts in PDF documents

If you send someone a document and the font you used isn't installed on their computer, it has to guess at a substitute to use instead, mucking up your design. PDF (Adobe's Portable Document Format) is great because the font information is included in the document file, so it displays as designed on any computer.

A font on your computer has a technical property called embedding permission, with four possible levels from full permission to no embedding allowed. The no embedding option is pretty rare, but I always like to check because I once built a design around a font that wouldn't embed and had to redo it. In Windows 7 you can check this through Control panel > Fonts.
A downloadable utility on Microsoft's Typography pages helped with earlier versions of Windows. Other software may let you see this property directly.

White space

Using too little space is one of the most basic mistakes of layout. Confronting the reader with a wall of text may scare them off, because reading it is hard work. So we break it up into paragraphs, and use headings to organise it to help them find their way around and structure the info as it goes into their head. For that to work, and to look attractive so they want to try reading it, there needs to be enough space around and between the elements on the page.

In particular, **headings** need space above and below so the eye can clearly differentiate sections of text. It's the visual equivalent of taking a breath. If you cram it all together it looks awful.

The same applies if you use **columns** of text: leave a decent space between them, so the eye can comfortably differentiate between them.

At the other end of the scale, don't leave massive swathes of white space unless you're going for a very stylised layout. Readers may interpret it as wasteful.

Alignment and justification

The easiest version to read is **left-aligned text**, sometimes called ragged-right. Because the line ends form an irregular shape, the eye has landmarks for keeping track of where it's got to.

Justified text, where both ends of a row align, is nice and neat and a good choice in some situations. However, if there's lots of it that's not well broken up, it's a more difficult and tedious read (especially with wider columns). Also, layout software handles the justification by stretching spaces between letters and words to make the text fit the space, and that sometimes leads to unsightly gappiness.

Justified text is also subject to **line end hyphenation**, which I hate with a passion. To make the lines fit, the software breaks a word in the middle and runs it over two lines. This leads to some hor-
rible artefacts. You should be able to turn it off in your design software's style settings.

As to **right-aligned** text, it can be useful as an occasional artistic touch but not for any substantial blocks of text. The reader's brain, trained to read left to right, can't find the line starts in a predictable place and doesn't have ragged line ends for landmarks.

Double space between sentences

This one polarises people! It's a relic of manual typewriters, where the letters were all on the same size of block, and hitting the space bar twice made for a better appearance. If you were trained that way so it became your habit, of course it's difficult to be told different.

However... computer programs like word processors and desktop publishers have a lot of stuff going on behind the scenes to adjust the spacing between letters, words and sentences to make things look good. If you put in a double space it can make a block of text look gappy. Can you see the difference here? It's more obvious for some typefaces than others. And for goodness' sake don't use multiple spaces *within* sentences!

A hail of bullets

If you want to make a list of things, the traditional way is to use colons and semicolons like this: apples; oranges; kiwi fruit; rhubarb. That's correct, but beyond a short list of short items it becomes hard work to read and interpret correctly. A bullet list overcomes that, and modern layout uses bullets a lot. It's a nice visual way to present information: point, point, point. But only with good layout. You need to put a bit of extra line space between bullets to make them visually distinct, rather than a solid block with spots.

As far as formatting bullets, it's important to be consistent. A former employer had this style rule: if each point stands as a sentence in its own right, start each with a capital and end it with a full stop; but if they follow as if they were parts of a sentence, start each with a small letter and end only the last one with a stop.

See how that works with our list of examples:

- apples
- oranges
- kiwi fruit
- rhubarb.

It's only one way to do it, and you'll sometimes have to make tricky judgement calls, but it's a baseline to work from.

By the way, don't overuse colons when introducing bullet lists. You can usually lead with a statement instead if you want, like "Here is a list of examples." Too much exotic punctuation flying around can make a paragraph look a bit weird and scary.

Teeny tiny text

A few years back I had an eye problem that affected the detail vision on one side. I was fortunate to come out of it with only a minor downgrade. But that time changed my thinking in a number of ways, and one of those was a new empathy for people with visual impairments.

So you may imagine how much I shout at the screen when perhaps half of the websites I see set the basic body text size *too damn small.*

Seriously. Perhaps a lot of online content is created by young hip people with perfect eyesight. But perhaps you've heard that we're all getting older? And there are more older people in the population? A sizeable proportion of people experience loss of detail vision as they get older: it's called age-related macular degeneration (AMD), and is estimated to affect one in 50 people over 50 years of age, and up to one in five people over the age of 85 (source: BBC Health website). Of course, there are all sorts of health issues that can affect the eyes of people of any age.

So your teeny tiny text is discrimination against older users. And the rest of us with imperfect human peepers!

Test your site in popular browser software. Set the zoom to 100% and make sure, at least, that someone with average vision can read it comfortably for minutes at a time. Remember also that users have all different sorts of computer set-ups: maybe you have a big, hi-res screen, but they might not.

If you're using a content management system like WordPress, avoid using display themes that set the text size too small. If you already have a theme and it won't let you make the text big enough, I really think it might be worth changing your site design.

Do you think people will hang around to look at a site that makes their eyes ache, or click off to visit the competition?

Oh, and never, ever, set up a website so that the user is unable to alter the text size in their browser settings. The label for setting stuff up so that people with different needs can use it is "**accessibility**". For websites, adjustable text size is one of the most basic things to get right. Another is colour combinations: low contrast between text and background makes it hard to read, and some combos are just crazy, like primary red on primary blue, where the text can appear to float in space and is hard for the eye to get a lock on.

I've focused on websites because they are particular offenders, but of course you should watch out for teeny tiny text in print, PDF and other formats too.

E-verywhere: the portable device revolution

You may not like or understand computing technology. Of course that's fine; but new developments are conquering the world with you or without you. I think now you're obliged to at least be *aware* of them if you're creating written content.

One major change of the last couple of years is the growth of portable devices: first smartphones, then e-readers like Amazon's Kindle, and now tablet PCs. Apple's iPad kickstarted the tablet market, and still dominates it, but now there are loads of companies producing devices. The latest wave to watch is the rise of lower-cost tablets using the Android operating system. Tech heavyweights Amazon and Google have launched 7-inch tablets, marketed for media consumption, and unfamiliar manufacturers from the far east sell basic tablets for around £100. In terms of access to technology, communication and media functions, that's incredible to a lad like me who saw the first personal computers as a schoolboy.

This trend isn't going away, because it turns information technology into a consumer product. People want the goodies it can give them, without getting snarled up in how the stuff actually works.

Now the hardware has reached a point where it can store and play loads of media and info, and we can carry that around with us to access whenever we like. At the same time, the app model of software lets us tap a button and see weather info or buy books, presented in a way that's optimised for that function.

I think this has now got enough momentum that when you're creating information products you have to assume that some users will be viewing them on portable devices and design accordingly.

If your users, clients and colleagues are even slightly gadget-friendly and well-off, they've probably already got at least one portable device they use for accessing media stuff. If you travel by public transport you can see lots of them. Some organisations are already issuing tablets to staff as computer kit: for instance a visit to the London Book Fair showed me that the publishing industry has really embraced the iPad.

This also creates new markets for content. People tried to push reflowable text ebooks for years, but it was a minority interest until the Kindle took off. As I write, Amazon UK has announced that it's now selling more ebooks than print books. By working directly with online sellers, authors can get a much greater proportion of cover price than in the traditional publishing process. Many price their ebooks at just a couple of pounds or dollars, looking for sales volume.

There is a flipside: some people think traditional bookstores could become a thing of the past in many places, as the loss of sales to digital makes it even harder to keep them viable.

Practicalities

What this means in practice will evolve over the next few years, but here are some things to think about if you want to produce content for portable devices.

In what format(s) will you release your content? It could be web pages, PDF documents, ebooks in EPUB format or Amazon's MOBI... What software or services will you need to create this?

Will it be a reflowable text ebook, like a novel on the Kindle? The user sets the text size and the software flows the text into screenfuls. Or will it be a fixed layout like a PDF?

If it's fixed layout, what page size will you work to, and what text size will you use? You want at least basic readability without zooming in. That means making text bigger relative to the page than you might for print. You can do that by making the text a bit larger, or by making the page size smaller – maybe Trade (6 x

9 inch) rather than the standard A4 (or Letter in the USA). I suggest that both larger text and smaller pages are going to become more common. It's natural to aim for one layout that'll work OK in both print and electronic editions, to minimise the extra work.

"Responsive web design" is a hot new thing at the moment – making pages that adapt well to different screen sizes and formats. If you have a website, make sure it looks OK on different devices and in different browser software.

Keeping off the rocks

Common mistakes to avoid

English is weird

It’s not regular and predictable. It’s sneaky and changeable, and likes to trip you up. But we forgive it this because it's a flexible and powerful tool, and at its best can be very beautiful.

The downside is that you have to learn how to use it properly, and that includes a lot of specific niggly stuff. This part of the book contains a selection of points where I’ve noticed people often go astray. See how many you already know. Maybe there are some new ones you can spot in your own writing and steer round in future.

If you want more of this detailed stuff, there are many fine books that go further into it. I’ve also found the *Guardian* newspaper’s style guide, freely available on its website, a useful resource: some stuff is right vs wrong, and some is the paper’s chosen way of doing things (and even when I disagree I can usually learn something).

Grammar and structure

Creepy capitals

Some people write with Capital letters appearing at the beginnings of Words all over the place, or randomly thrown in. I guess that's because they've never quite got the rules for this and are playing it safe. Never capitalise a word unless you have a reason to.

- The start of a sentence always takes a capital.
- Proper nouns are official titles of things, denoting status or perhaps brand recognition, and they take capitals. So Amazon (company), or the Amazon (river), or President Obama, or the Department of Health. A person's job title is one, though a *description* of their role is not: so you could say, "Ms Smith is a finance officer", or, "This is Jill Smith, Finance Officer".

Whether you capitalise each word within a headline is, to some degree, a style issue – but it usually looks better if you don't use caps after the first word, as if it were a sentence (but don't put a full stop or anything at the end).

Perilous plurals

You do not make a plural with an apostrophe. "Apple's £1.20/kg." A lot of people who actually know this find it creeping in if they let their guard down. Just stick "s" on the end of the word (or "es" if that won't work, or a few words are their own plurals, like "fish").

Apocalyptic apostrophes

These most troublesome of punctuation marks do two jobs.

- They denote possession – "Maria's submarine." That can also be more association than strict ownership, like "Bob's auntie", or even on the outer edges of abstractness "two days' work". If the owning word ends in "s", a good rule of thumb is to use apostrophe-s ("Stelios's rabbit") *or* just the apostrophe on its own if the result would look or sound horrible ("Stelios' rabbit"). If the owning word is plural, just put an apostrophe after the S: "the cats' toys".
- They signal that one or more letters have been left out. So "don't" is a shortened version of "do not". (It's not always logical, e.g. "shan't" for "shall not".)

Bothersome brackets

Round brackets (known as parentheses) are handy for additional information that stands apart from the main flow of the text. They indicate visually "you can go round this bit if you really want". Don't overuse them though – I certainly catch myself putting stuff in brackets when it could go perfectly well in the main text (in a new paragraph if necessary).

If the text in brackets stands alone as a sentence, its full stop goes in the brackets with it. If the text is part of another sentence, use that sentence's full stop.

- (The cat sat on the mat.)
- I walked over to the cat (it sat on the mat).

Colon irritation

This is more advanced punctuation, and a good rule of thumb is to use it as little as possible, especially if you tend to get it mixed up.

The **colon**, one dot above another, is basically a big pause in a sentence that joins two clauses together. It's used for introducing a following idea, or explaining something more fully. "He threw up his hands: the punctuation was a nightmare." If you can make it two separate sentences instead, that's often clearer and punchier. In British English the colon is followed by a small letter, as it's the same sentence. (In American English, commonly followed style guidelines say colons should be followed by a capital letter. To me it looks awful and is confusing because it looks like a sentence start.)

The **semicolon**, a dot above a comma, is a longer comma for when you need a bigger pause in the way the sentence reads. It can be useful for lists, especially where the items themselves contain commas. "Noah checked off the last animals: penguins, filed under birds; flamingos, filed under hatstands; and platypuses, swept under the carpet."

A singular organisation

If you refer to an organisation, there's only one of it. So the surrounding words need to be singular, not plural. The plural comes in when you talk about the people *in* the organisation as a group.

There can be a strong impulse to do it the wrong way – I think this is because we know organisations are made of people and, being social animals, want to recognise them. Often people are so conflicted that they mix both together in the same sentence, like "The council has announced that they will be providing unicycles for public use" – the worst of all worlds.

Sometimes you may need to tweak the sentence structure to make the singular words sound natural, even though they're correct.

- Universal Exports *are* hosting an event. *Wrong.*
- Universal Exports *is* hosting an event. *Right.*
- Universal Exports' employees *are* going to an event. *Right.*
- Mr Bond *is* going to an event. *Right. Licence to edit reinstated.*

I and me

"Can you give Bob and I some feedback?" is wrong. Break it down and see what makes sense. "Can you give Bob some feedback?" – fine so far. "Can you give I some feedback?" – clearly it ought to be "me" rather than I. You give it to Bob and to me. Turning it round, "Bob and I have received feedback" is correct.

-ise and –ize

The alternate endings for all those words like recognise/recognize. In British English, in most cases, either is correct so you can choose. Personally I dislike the Z version, so when I'm in sole control of material I change it to the S (part of my personal style guide; and the Guardian's too). In American English –ize is standard.

Splitting infinitives

This refers to putting other words between a verb and its "to", the granddaddy of all examples being Star Trek's, "To boldly go where no man has gone before." (Authentic 1960s sexist version!) People have often taught that this is a bad thing to do. In fact, authorities generally recognise that there isn't anything wrong with it, grammar-wise.

The *problem* is all those people who tie their sentences in knots to avoid it, producing ugly stuff like, "Boldly to go where no man has gone before." If you want a corrected version, put the adverb after the verb it describes: "To go boldly where no man has gone before."

Putting words together to make adjectives

For instance "follow-up report". They usually take a hyphen to show that the words have become a linked concept. Leaving the words separate can sometimes be ambiguous, like "man eating tiger".

Words and phrases

Affect and effect. To affect is to influence or change someone or something. (It can also mean to put on, pretend, feign – like "She affected outrage, but I knew the truth.") An effect is a result or change produced by some influence. (You *can* use effect as a verb, meaning something like achieve or accomplish: "He effected a quick getaway.") A mix-up like "The revelation had a surprising affect" is wrong.

All toothpastes are not the same. That actually means no toothpastes are the same. The usual intention is to say that some things are different and stand out from the field, for which you need "*Not all* toothpastes are the same." For a sparkly fresh grammar you'll like.

Complement is when things go well together and enhance each other or make a complete whole. **Compliment** is when you say something is nice. **Complimentary** is something given away for free. "I complimented her on the way the complimentary towel complemented her figure."

Comprises means "is made up of". "The package comprises of the following items" is wrong: you don't need the "of" because it's already built in. "The package comprises the following items" is correct. Think of it like "includes" (which, as a more commonly used word, may be a better choice in some cases).

Dependent/dependant. The first describes the state of depending, and the second refers to the person or thing that depends. "Do you have any dependants?" "Well, I suppose Mr Snuffly is dependent on me."

Foreword. This is the bit you see at the front of books, often by a guest introducing the author's work. It's the *words* that go *before* the main text. Sometimes there's an "afterword" at the end. I'm mentioning it because I've seen it rendered as "Forward", presumably a misunderstanding of how it sounds, rather than a command to charge; and also as "Foreward", an indecisive hybrid that isn't a word at all.

Formally/formerly. "Formally" means doing things the proper/official way. Even if the Queen is your mate you probably still greet her formally in public. "Formerly" is about stuff that used to be the case. "Her Majesty was formerly on good terms with Mr Gray, but feels that 'Yo Liz!' was an inappropriate form of address."

Its and it's. "It's" always indicates missing letters, shortening "it is" or "it has". The possessive, "belonging to it", is always "its" with no apostrophe. It's a pain.

Lead (*leed*) is a verb for bringing followers along with you. The past tense is **led** – "I led the horse to water but couldn't make him drink." The similar-sounding **lead** (*ledd*) is just for heavy metal fans.

Literally. An adjective used to reinforce that you really do mean exactly what you're saying. So the conversational gambit, "When she said that I literally died!", actually means, "I have joined the ranks of the undead; go for your shotgun."

Must've, should've, would've, could've. Those versions with apostrophes are abbreviations for "must have", etc. There's a tendency for people to hear the sound and get the wrong end of the stick, adopting "You must *of* known it was wrong!", which is wrong. "You must *have* known it was wrong!" is right.

Onto. There is no "onto"! You can use "in to", "into" (to do with the inside of something, like "looking into the room"), or "on to".

Practice is a noun, and **practise** is a verb. "I practise playing the bagpipes every night. Though the neighbours insist I don't need the practice." It's the same for **licence** (the thing) and **license** (the action).

Principal is a primary thing, like the head of a college, or the amount of money you initially invest. Used as an adjective it means main, or most important: "The principal reason for writing this book...". A **principle** is a rule or underpinning: that could be factual, like "three principles of the combustion engine", or an ethical standard, like, "The man is an unprincipled liar!" You can get back to first principles; or say someone is a man/woman of principle. You could write an ethics essay about the principal principle.

Programme is the British spelling of a planned sequence of activities; but it's the convention to use the American spelling, **program**, to refer to computer software.

Proven. Very common, but in most cases the past tense of "prove" should be "proved".

Quality. In the sense of "Quality furniture at great prices!" Technically this is meaningless. What quality does it have? "Smelly" is a quality. "High quality" is a shorthand for "good materials and workmanship"; or you can get specific about which great properties your stuff has, and catch people who are looking for those keywords. Like "expert pedantry".

Trying. "Try and write an article" is wrong. The correct version is "Try *to* write an article". (The first implies two separate things: you're going to try and you're going to write.)

The wicked which. In most cases you should use "that". It's the standard way of defining properties of things: "The bag *that I brought with me* is heavy." "Which" is for clauses giving additional information: they can often be removed without losing the core meaning. So you could reword to "The bag, *which I brought with me*, is heavy" to reflect that you bringing it is just a bit of extra description. Of course "which" is also used for asking for a specific item out of all the possibilities: "Which bag did you bring?" "That one."

Who and whom. My personal view is that "whom" is an awkward bit of language that's on its way out, and good riddance. You can usually switch a sentence round to sound natural with just "who". However, technically it's still correct to use "whom" to agree with "them/him/her" rather than "they/he/she". "To whom is it addressed?" Just make a sentence that doesn't sound awkward if you read it out.

Who's and whose. The first is a contraction of "who is" or "who has". The second is used to talk about possession, either asking or describing. "Who's a pretty boy then? Hey, whose parrot is this?" "It belongs to my room-mate whose gran runs a pet shop."

"**It bugs me to no end**", means "without purpose". "It bugs me no end", means without limit.

“**I could care less**”, means I haven’t reached the limit of my ability to give a damn, which is precisely not the point of the original, “I *couldn’t* care less”.

“**Get off of my lawn**” is redundant, repetitious and horrible. “Get off my lawn” covers it.

Bah!

Arrival

I hope you've enjoyed that gallop through the subject! We've covered:

- principles of writing to communicate
- style and process
- writing persuasively
- layout and design
- common mistakes to avoid.

You might want to make yourself a list of a few points that you particularly want to work on in your writing. You can also note some areas where you're doing well already – great! (But remember to be honest about your skills!) Don't just listen to me: check out resources like plain English guides that'll give help where you want it.

This is an ongoing process, like developing other skills. Take it a bit at a time, and aim for a target that suits you. Maybe you want to be good; or maybe you want to be good *enough*, using it to support your key strengths.

The result should be that more of your message bottles reach their intended islands. That can only benefit us all. We've been waiting to hear from you.

End notes

Sources

Influencer; Kerry Patterson, Joseph Grenny, David Maxfield; Ron McMillan; Al Switzler; McGraw-Hill; 2008

The Guardian style guide – one of the UK's national papers has its own style guide online at www.guardian.co.uk/styleguide

Acknowledgments

To all the pieces of writing I've worked on, for the practice.

To my former colleagues at Citizens Advice, for an environment that kicked my thinking about editing and information presentation into a higher gear. I'm still not going to proofread anybody's emails!

To the Inspired Entrepreneur community for feedback and encouragement.

Most of all, to Valerie Gray, my Mum, who taught me to read and started the whole thing. Thanks for everything, chuck.

About the author

Tim Gray is an English writer, editor, self-publisher, finer world advocate and amateur-league geek. Rocketed from the exploding planet Huddersfield as a youngster, he now lives in Nottingham and attempts to use his powers for good.

He has a knack for clear, concise writing and a really annoying level of attention to detail. His ~~victims~~ achievements have included environmental newsletters, roleplaying game books, websites, training materials – and now ebooks!

Find out more at www.yourclear.info.

Lightning Source UK Ltd.
Milton Keynes UK
UKOW032352050413

208752UK00008B/257/P

9 780957 457201